A Most Terrible and Deadly Season
Poems of War

A Most Terrible and Deadly Season
Poems of War

by

Mikel Vause

Cover design by Shay Culligan
Cover photograph by Jerry Nelson

ISBN: 978-1-954353-41-1

Kelsay Books
502 South 1040 East, A-119
American Fork, Utah, 84003

First and foremost, I wish to thank my wife, Janis, and my children, Kelly, Emily, Sarah, and Jared for their unflinching support for over forty years. Any success I've had is due, in the most part, to them.

To all those members of the armed forces worldwide who willingly give their all in the philosophies of freedom and liberty.

What we now need to discover in the social realm is the moral equivalent of war; something heroic that will speak to man as universally as war does, and yet will be as compatible with their spiritual selves as war has proved to be incompatible.
—William James

War means tears to thousands of mothers eyes
When their sons go to fight
And lose their lives
—Edwin Starr

We are spinning our own fates, good or evil, never to be undone.
—William James

War is what happens when language fails.
—Margaret Atwood

I know not with what weapons World War III will be fought, but World War IV will be fought with sticks and stones.
—Albert Einstein

The true soldier fights not because he hates what is in front of him, but because he loves what is behind him.
—G.K. Chesterton

War must be, while we defend our lives against a destroyer who would devour all; but I do not love the bright sword for its sharpness, nor the arrow for its swiftness, nor the warrior for his glory. I love only that which they defend.
—J.R.R. Tolkien

It is forbidden to kill; therefore all murderers are punished unless they kill in large numbers and to the sound of trumpets.
—Voltaire

Only the dead have seen the end of war.
—Plato

There are perhaps many causes worth dying for, but to me, certainly, there are none worth killing for.
—Albert Dietrich

A small but noteworthy note. I've seen so many young men over the years who think they're running at other young men. They are not. They are running at me.
—Markus Zusak

If you win, you need not have to explain ... If you lose, you should not be there to explain!
—Adolf Hitler

Listen up—there's no war that will end all wars.
—Haruki Murakami

Never think that war, no matter how necessary, nor how justified, is not a crime.
—Ernest Hemingway

What difference does it make to the dead, the orphans and the homeless, whether the mad destruction is wrought under the name of totalitarianism or in the holy name of liberty or democracy?
—Mahatma Gandhi

All war is a symptom of man's failure as a thinking animal.
—John Steinbeck

Contents

Harry Patch

For a more sacred place for the British does not exist in the world.
—Winston Churchill in 1919

Ferocious memories
Victory great loss,
Constant shelling churned
Clay soil smashed drainage systems.
Most rain since Noah's flood
Chaos, with mud so deep
Men horses drowned
Swallowed by Mother Earth
Still clear in mind's eye.
Hundred years won't wash away
Trauma experience
Lost friends young soldiers
Marooned in bowels of sadness
Once each year
Solitary prayer for fallen friends
Cried by a last man
Standing

* Harry Patch was the last British survivor of the battle of Ypres. He died in 2009 at the age of 111.

Topaz Mountain

for Setsoko and Simon Winchester

An alkali land of sagebrush
    tumble weeds and dust storms
Apart from civilization
     encircled by mountains snowcapped and distant
     only the most resilient plant or animal
     can thrive such deathly isolation
Land of the Samurai
    of cherry blossoms
    and rising sun
    Bonzai trees precise
    sculpted transcendent
Testament to the elements
    Earth Fire Water Wind
    wed to beauty
     Orange Omanthus and Carnation
    flush of Cherry and Peach
Balanced harmony
    morning Glory and Violet
    yesterday's reflections
    Camellia explosion of red
    tempered by yellow pistils
Window to tomorrow
     cosmos and Chrysanthemum
    alive in the present
Dust swirls and blanks out the sun
    children new from American West's
    coastal rain forests
    rich soil for farms and flowers
A paradox to young minds
    how different is the earth
    with the war it seems unforgiving
    punishment of the innocent
    guileless children obeisant adults

Citizen Prisoners in a free land
   removed to desolation
   a protection for other free citizens
   skin color and the shape of eyes
   the qualifier for detention
America's dark days
   slavery paradoxically emancipation
   massacre of Indians
   Japanese concentration camps
   stolen freedom in a free land.

Christmas at Rocco's

1

A chorus of ghosts sing
And memories recklessly rush
Knocking about my cranial attic
Rattling eyes
Attempt to escape

Different
Fascinated by uncommon things
Places people languages experiences

WWII ended
Camp Ogden's gates opened
German Italian POW's
Spilled out to be returned
To homelands scarred pocked
A record of war

Rocco Colantonio stepped out
Savored fresh sweet air
Mountains still capped
With late spring snow
Alpine breezes mix
With wildflowers and sage

East-West troop trains
Wait restless at Union Station
Sixty hours to New York shipyards
Ships carry POW's to Europe

2

War over
Open sores festering
Hard to forgive
In war no exemption
Pain for some is
Quick then fades
Others suffer for days
Months years lifetimes
Camp Ogden held
POW's German Italian
Captured doing their duty
For king and country
As with our boys
Mostly uniform color
Separated them

Homesickness gnaws gut soul
Hungry for home
Mothers young girlfriends
Wives children
Rivers mountains planted fields
Vineyards winding ancient cobbled
Pathways dark and cool

Dear dreams
In mind's eye
Joy bolstered blurry hindsight
Hope tarnished polish
Hides scratches dints
Patina clouds silver

A funhouse mirror
Twists stretches
Funny eyes and stomach bulge
Mood turns terrible monstrous
Ugly reflection
Real not fantasy

3

Home in Italy
Exploded by bombs
Excreted from the bowels
Of B-52's
Sorrow filled heart
Village folks sadly aged
Friends who know
Village changed
Family masked
Sadness defeat
Not much to build on
Odd jobs
Embassy lines.
Careless bureaucrats
Transplants from America
A land of plenty

West bound train from New York
Led to Ogden by way
Of new lands big rivers
Forest fields farms
Vast open space

Painful uncertain
Alone a new land
Of his war-time enemy
Held him prisoner

His journey ends in Ogden
In the lap of his captors
He was different
Wielder machinist like Dad
Stumbled with English
Brockton Block Buster looks
Wavy black hair
Heavy whiskers olive skin
Dad gave him work

His foothold in America
A clapboard shack
On Pennsylvania Avenue
Trains shook windows
Steel wheels scream
Thunder by twice a day

Married Rosa
An older Italian woman
Happy heavy round loud
Stiff dyed hair
Rouged wrinkled cheeks
Strong determined
Delivered a boy at sixty

4

Christmas week tradition
Dinner with Rocco and Rosa
Around cramped table
Overheated living room
Tree buried in aluminum icicles
Brothel red lights
Real Italian food
Fit for God

It was their way—gratitude
They loved to celebrate
Dad's kindness
Repaid by sacrifice
Every Christmas

5

Time passed trust and friendship grew
Rosa insisted would Dad
Deliver the eulogy
Tough old Rosa
Outlived him.
Twenty-five years

It fell to me to fulfill
My father's commitment
To honor Italian tradition
When her casket closed
A door closed on my childhood
And left me only memories

A Witness of Verdun

most terrible ordeal 4 days 4 nights
                    icy mud narrow trench relentless fire,

cracks separates iron will
                    gas clouds eyes

degraded prayers fall from
                    blue lips of skeletons

follow a blind commander
                    with tiny steps,

zigzagging as if drugged
                    these speechless faces

sing unbelievable horrors
                    of martyrdom....

Sweet Smoke

Fall air cold and clean
Leaves blaze red golden yellow
Early morning grass a sea
Of inverted icicles
Await obliteration with first sun
On ridge-lines clouds
Rest on mountains
A gray-white mantle
Apples hang crisp and ready

Still after fifty years I
See Mr. Rackham roll down
The ramp from the front door
Only to stop on the sidewalk
And light his cigar—a White Owl

He left his legs just outside Paris
In the spring mud of the Argonne Forest
Fighting under Black Jack Pershing
He advanced to help shatter
The Hindenburg Line
The Armistice not far off
He came home with a chest-full of medals
And a love of cigars

22

He'd strike a match on his overalls
And with his White Owl
Clenched between his teeth
Like bellows his cheeks
Puffed in and out until the end
Glowed red and aromatic clouds
Of tobacco smoke floated
Around his old stained felt hat

In a closed space
His house or tool shed
Coarse tobacco on fire would overcome
The most seasoned smoker
But wafting through autumn air
Mixed with compost and manure
A sweet comfort
I wonder if his brothers
In the French forest
Or to the German boys
Who too awaited possible death
When the bullets and bombs flew
Found solace in the scent

To a boy forty years on in America
His stories of young soldiers
Armed with rifles as big as they
Bayonets ready when the command
"Over the top" sent them
Through "no man's land"
In the "war to end all wars"
Were as rarified as Arthurian legend

War-torn France
So far from Utah
In distance and time
Yet in this space and time-warp
I'm there in the Argonne knee-deep in spring mud
With this legless man
And the sweet smoke

Old Papers

*...and the blood of the innocent shall stand as a witness against them, yea, and
cry mightily against them at the last day.*

—Alma 14:11

*Let every man remind their descendants that they also are soldiers who must
not desert the ranks of their ancestors, or from cowardice fall behind.*

—Plato

Old papers tell stories
"Perry at the Pole!"
"Black Tuesday"
"The Great Depression"
"The Kingfisher Dead"
"Mantel Slams Record HR"
ups and downs of life
Yin and Yang of existence

Raised on a sheep ranch
outside Malad
daughter of Welsh immigrants
she knew well
the struggle to survive
isolation loneliness cold
books newspapers
brought the world
to sage brush hills

Now dead twenty-seven years
mother left little
poems recipes letters
knickknacks photographs
news clippings on the fridge
coupon dishes from General Mills

half dozen wigs
after years of chemo
she waited death quietly
household in order

In her important prized things
rolled up tied with string
Ogden newspapers
yellowed headlines
twentieth century watermarks
November 11, 1918—Armistice Day
December 7, 1941—The Day of Infamy
May 8, 1945—V-E day
August 14, 1945—V-J day
July 27, 1953—Korean Armistice
January 23, 1973—Peace with Honor
August 2, 1990—Operation Desert Shield

She tracked war
through old newsprint
from birth to death
portal for learning
to remember not to forget
hope for harmony
protection prevention peace
prayer for the present
prediction prescription prophecy
for the future

Knife Man

I don't look at a knife the way I used to. I'm more aware of what it is. I think twice. This is a key finger. It's in every chord.
—Neil Young

Mr. Sparks ate lard—Morrell Pure Snow-Cap
Out of blue can on his bread
Habit of hard times
War years and Depression
Hard on him legs gone
Blown off in France
In his old shed
He made knives to get by

Young boy old neighborhood
I'd hang around watch
He'd spend hours
Wheelchair moving
Lathe to grinder to drill press
Broken band saw blades
Hold an edge
Blade shapes in soapstone

Not like a Buck or Case
Utilitarian work knives
None better to slice
Bacon or side pork or cured ham
For morning meat
Dad Mr. Sparks' knife in hand
Would head to the tool shed

Fifty years since Dad died
Same for Mr. Sparks
I still have one of his
Sawblade knives
Elk antler handle
Sharp enough to shave with

Morrigan*

All Ravens are crows
Not all crows are Ravens

Old crow watching hungrily, from his perch in yonder tree
                                        —Dave Mallet

There's little difference
Between Ravens and crows
According to myth
Their glossy black presence
Is required at the Tower to protect
The monarchy—Clipped wings the Crown's insurance

It's a Raven that taps and raps
In Poe's 108 lines of iambic pentameter
Melancholy harbinger of death and despair
Scavengers pick deadlights from boney sockets
To carry away lost love

A murder of crows
Search for carrion
Frequent visitors with Death
On battlefield in cemeteries
Their caw a message from God
Or the netherworld

Beady-eyed intellectuals
Gather to decide capital fate of another
Strength in numbers
Distress calls bring protection
From horned owls red-tailed hawks raccoons
Faithful—no adultery among crows

They circle above cutting
Sunlight then shadows
Eyes to their fortunes
To snatch newly sown seeds
Or as with the way of all flesh
Turn death to life

* Black crows symbolize the Welsh goddess of war and death, Morrigan.

A Most Terrible and Deadly Season

I feel strong for the battle, but I know every ounce of strength will be wanted.
                        —Base Camp 1924, George Leigh Mallory

Everest is a matter of universal of human endeavor, a cause from which there is no withdrawal, whatever losses it may demand.
                                        —G.O. Dyrenfurth

It's human to go out
Since the beginning of days
To leave casual collective comfort,
Escape the jail-house of society
Explore on the fringes of existence—
(Both physical and metaphysical),
Touch the dark spots on the map
Search for freshness
Investigate lost innocence
Lean against the wind
Scratch the surface of iron-hard ice
Taunt tendons, cramped muscle
Grasp cold rock—dig for razor-sharp flakes
War once fulfilled instinctual urge
Price was high
Shackleton fought a war of adventure
Armed only with physical toughness
And creativity
No mortars or Mustard Gas
Only cold isolation
And open water in a small boat.
Standard then was set
What was said about history repeating itself?
The gauntlet was thrown
On Everest in 1996—It was
A most terrible and deadly season

Paradox

For Jared

Ask not for whom the bell tolls…
          —John Donne

From high school at seventeen
Age no issue for friends
Four years either side okay
Vietnam was in full swing—a police action
Should have been over before it started
Drug on sixteen years
"The Lottery" assigned
Boys eighteen numbers 1 to 366
Random birthdays
Rather than gamble
Some joined or sought deferments

At seventeen I wanted to be a Marine
Dad's cousin was a WWI Marine
Not old enough for cigarettes or the vote
And military service only
By mother's permission—she refused
She loved America—her brother
Was amphibious tank man in the South Pacific
He was gone six years
Wounded severely
If drafted I should go
Not volunteer

Thayne Bowen innocent boy
Her nephew was called up 1944
Four weeks learning war
Then off to enlist
Lasted four days

Her first letter came back stamped deceased
Came back to her days
Before the official telegram
Reached his folks

My status 1-A lottery number sixty-two
1971 monthly quotas two hundred
Nineteen I understood Vietnam
Hated its politics
I deferred for two years in Missouri—church work
I was lucky the draft missed me
Or maybe I'm a coward
Guilty because three neighbor boys died there

2014
War in the Persian Gulf
Iran Iraq Afghanistan Yemen Syria
My son Apache Black Hawk
Door gunner and medic
A patriot loves the Army

A Last Call for Young Men

Under the level winter sky
I saw a thousand Christs go by.
They sang an idle song and free
As they went up to Calvary.
                    —Marjorie Pickthall

A whistle screams harsh and shrill rips the air
A last call for young men
Traveling to the future
Long goodbyes of days and hours press into seconds
Emotions freeze no time for laughter or tears
Fresh-faced boys full of anticipation
Hearts and minds fueled with adrenalin
Adventurous dreams light the path toward manhood
Off in service of God and King

From the ships conscripted to carry troops who
In neat rows and straight lines march in cadence to battle
Marquess of Queensbury sense of honor and fair play
Young officers on spirited horseback sabers flashing
Eager to prove themselves brave unflinching leaders
Antiquated strategies imbedded in tradition
Send this army ten abreast across acres of mud
Crisscrossed with trenches and barbed wire
Marching in the footsteps of a dozen centuries of conquest

It's different this time
Going from trench to trench
Crawling through mud blood and body parts
Still recognizable still baring the taunt skin of youth
Remains of boys in uniform just like them
Who just hours before sought to be tested
To seek in vain for glory and honor on the field of Flanders
They died in vast numbers unlike any time in history

Gas powered machine guns spit bullets lightning fast
Soldiers drop line after line as red hot lead
Tears and shreds young bodies
Mortar-fire with tennis racket pops rains down
Death-whistle of rockets break through cloud covered sky from
Miles off-shore
Gas blinds eyes blisters skin chokes lungs
So many die alone to drown in mud
Confused by death where is the glory

Keepsakes stripped from blood filled pockets
Of green wool that smells of gunpowder and fear
Relics of a young life
Tied up in a handkerchief monogrammed with blood and tears
All that's left to return to sad families
Bodies shattered and broken like childhood dreams
Lay scattered in a foreign field

Unfulfilled and without explanation
Words scatter like shrapnel broadcast in fragments
Voices child-like cry for mother between
The rattle of guns and the roar of artillery
Uncertain fingers claw painfully at the air
Confusion reaches helplessly into nothing
And seeks to escape the horror
No one told them how to die
Death in real terms was not discussed in training
An abstraction that applies only to the enemy
Other young men dressed in gray uniforms
So when it visits our boys it's hard to comprehend
Death is something that happens to others

So much is lost in battle
If the genius of those dead could mature
How different the world might be
There's no equation to measure such loss
An oxymoron "the war to end all wars"
A paradox to sell—a bad idea
An unfulfillable proposition
Because of greed lust for power
War never be shelved or cast off
It will continue to lurk in genetic memory
Like Satan's Angels hovering ready
To explode and shatter all tomorrows

It Was a Yard Sale

European nations began World War I with a glamorous vision of war, only to be psychologically shattered by the realities of the trenches. The experience changed the way people referred to the glamour of battle; they treated it no longer as a positive quality but as a dangerous illusion.
—Virginia Poster

It was a yard sale
Mr. Moulding died
everything going cheap
I saw a lamp
next to his favorite chair

An artillery shell wired for light
souvenir from the Great War
brass shell casing hammered
in a quiet time
a rose—a fleur-de-lis—"France 1913–1918"

Wintertime the mud of Flanders fields
froze turned trenches to ice boxes
boys endured mud trench-foot disease
forced to face frostbite's putrid black flesh

Cold slowed will to fight
joints stiffen blood gets thick
yearns for summer sun
that causes the unburied dead
to swell bloat rot
fouls blue skies and flowers

Nature's frigid truce allows men's minds rest
shell and bullet casings decorated
figures carved from wood and bone
sketches scratched in chalk
on rocky outcrops around dug-outs
art confirmed their existence in the battle zone.

Tragic art at high cost is lost
cast off at yard sales
or to collect dust at Goodwill
messages from the killing fields
of the "war to end all wars"
lost to the future.

Cold War

It was always there
Yellow air-raid siren
Standing tall above the fire station
On 4th Street
Several times a month
It would let loose
A chalk-board scratching scream
And we'd practice civil defense drills.
By hiding under our desks
Or lining the school hallways
Ducking under the ancient coat hooks and shelves
Leaving us to wonder about the future

In winter our elementary playground covered
With the "greatest snow on earth"
Sparkling in the bright Utah sun
Teachers said it sparkled because radiation
From bomb tests in Nevada
Filled cold and fresh tasting snow
Eating it would cause cancer

The world was a dangerous place
Even in Ogden, Utah
Mountain home of the Mormons
And the military
Where the "house of Israel" would
According to Isaiah
Learn peace and dwell forever

The bright blue of the Rocky Mountain sky
A perfect dome of heaven
Cloudless and sunlit
Scarred by vapor trail
Its divine stillness broken
Only by sparrows and fighter jets
Peace shattered by bird song and sonic booms

A Hundred Years

It's been a hundred years
Since Owen wrote "Dulce et Decorum Est"*
When young men were left to die
In mud-filled trenches

A hundred years poison gas choked lungs
Blinded eyes pushed yellow clouds through
Open mouths and nostrils to suffocate brains
And leave behind madness or death

A hundred years wounded were laid in fields
Cried for home and mother
Begged for relief suffered from lost limbs
Faces shot away or burned to wrinkled leather

A hundred years that poppies push through
Shell pocked mud seeds hidden for decades
Recalled from suspended animation
To dance in sunlight and blue sky

* It's great and glorious to die for one's country.

Over There

Johnnie, get your gun ...
Make your daddy glad
To have had such a lad.
Tell your sweetheart not to pine,
To be proud her boy's in line.
Over there, over there,
Send the word ... that the Yanks are coming...
      —George M. Cohan

Early mornings
headed to the bus stop
Earl passed our kitchen window
Key overalls cotton work shirt
denim jacket big patch pockets
he was in uniform

Sometimes he'd stop
fingers cracked with time to roll a smoke
shake Bull Durham tobacco
into onion-skin cigarette paper
age-coated tongue sealed the gummed edge

I asked to learn to roll smokes
steer clear of tobacco boy
he wrapped a paper over his comb
put it to his mouth
played it like a kazoo
said I learned that in the war

Earl was a dough boy
did his bit
in the forests of France
shattered by cannon fire
earth matted pocked scarred
too young to know better
bullets held no terror

Mechanized military insanity
no weakness tolerated
land and spirit plundered
a marriage of horror and suffering
blood ether gangrene
order of the day

Earl lived with death for a year
crawled through mud and body parts
young men just like him
skin ripped by barbed wire
turned black in frozen trenches
smoked cigarettes to hide the smell

He was never the same after 1918
he tended his garden and fruit trees
baked pies at Ross and Jack's on 25th Street
never drove a car or went to church
his wife Millie burned the weeds in the ditch.

Neighbors

Along the headband
Of the rusty German helmet
Fifty-two ticks in white
Kill numbers
Just below the 50-caliber hole

Such impact
Would easily blow
A steel helmet
From the head
It was to protect

It came to my friend
From his father
A German solider
Who made America
His home after the war

Few neighbors
Knew Mr. Ruthstrom
Wore the Nazi uniform
Likely killed American boys
Protected by a stern and quiet life

Postcard perfect
All American
White house green shutters
Manicured lawns ruler straight edges
Fitzers fronted by red, pink, and white petunias

Karl worked on hot rods
'40 Willeys
Hopped up engine
Traction masters
Race-master Dragster slicks
Moon Eyes and Schneider Iron Cross decals

A few beers
wrong way on the I–15 ramp
Young mother three kids
Two friends dead
Like his father
Karl lived long enough
To know how many Americans
Died by his hand.

Old Ghosts

Quiet street
Old ghosts meet
Hollow eyes
Transfixed vision in reverse
Grief stricken sorrow
Vomiting dead youth
One day sixty thousand
And more died
In mindless slaughter
The Butcher* architect of defeat
Military autocrats
Plot in luxury well back
A war of attrition
Army on its back foot
Sea of churned earth
The blood of innocence
Frozen by fear
Tear-stained faces
Press against stone lined trench walls
Swallowing back the acid of doubt
Intimate reality—haunted
Wagner's Chorus of the Gods

* Field Marshall Lord Haig: He was nicknamed "Butcher Haig" for the two million British casualties endured under his command. The Canadian War Museum comments, "His epic but costly offensives at the Somme (1916) and Passchendaele (1917) have become nearly synonymous with the carnage and futility of First World War battles." (Wikipedia)

By Candlelight

By candlelight a pencil
scratches across rough paper
last lines before
"going over the top"

Air flooded with anticipation
and fear
the rattle of kit as soldiers
lift packs rifles loaded

Boys white with fear
tear streaked cheeks
some hide behind
profanity and bravado
eyes that can't hide concern

Shouts of sergeants
platoons line up
tin helmets give a false
sense of security

Orders filter down from generals
away from the front
secure in requisitioned villas
and hotels

They play a game of attrition
with young lives when
sending faceless boys to die
in rat filled trenches

By bullets bombs gas
neck-deep mud
In "No Man's Land"

We Were There

When I was small
My parents bought me books
My favorites came in a series entitled *We Were There* ...
We Were There at the Alamo
... with the Mayflower Pilgrims
... on the Oregon Trail
... with Byrd at the South Pole
... in the Klondike Gold Rush
... with Lewis and Clark
My favorite was *We Were There at the Opening of the Atomic Era.*
Little did I know living in Utah I really was *There.*
In elementary school we practiced air raid drills,
Every fire station had a yellow Civil Defense siren,
Buildings downtown, the library, and even some churches.
Were designated as fallout shelters.
People believed in limited nuclear war.
At recess, in the winter, teachers told us not to eat the fresh snow.
It sparkled from radiation that floated over Utah in clouds
From A-Bomb tests in Nevada.
From where I lived I couldn't see the flash,
Feel the earth shake,
Hear the explosion,
The sky wasn't dark from the terrible mushroom cloud,
Yet across the Great Basin sand melted to glass.

The Pier at Brighton

Behold, a ram caught in a thicket by its horns;
Offer the Ram of Pride instead of him.
But the old man would not so, but slew his son…
—Wilfred Owen

On the Sussex Riviera
Fashionable couples would,
In the crisp salt air of the Channel
Stroll arm in arm
Along the boardwalk
To dance under the Palace Pavilion.

But at Brighton beach,
During the war to end all wars,
When the wind was right,
And the sky clear,
And the Sun warm,
You could smell the bodies
Left lying on Flanders Field.

There was another war,
Not long before
That the dead Boers were left to lie in Sun
And suffer this same indignity
But Brighton was protected from that distant reality.

It's ironic that with this war,
Its theater only eighty-eight miles
As the crow flies from Palace Pier,
That the ocean breeze would
Carry the smell of corpses
To gay sands of Brighton.

In war,
Death dances with impunity
To the music of machine guns and airplanes
Waltzes in and out of clouds of Mustard Gas
And pauses only long enough
To choke the life and innocence
From a whole generation.

The Sun Never Sets on the British Empire

In Sussex there's poetry
Carried on ocean winds
If one listens closely
They'll taste smell
Words of Conan Doyle
Or Byron Kipling Hardy
Maybe Woolf or Austen
Sing out for careful ears
Like songs of Sirens tempt
One to walk out dark wooden pier
Sway as angry wind tears holes
Through black and gray clouds
Roll and tumble wrestling
To push open bursting bladders
Those who walk
On aged boards screwed
To piles pounded through sand
That reach bedrock a sense of safety
Those who brave uncertainty
Walk to its end
Stare into black bottomless sea
Rain blown sideways
Wood creeks rolls groans
Waves attack ancient constructs
Try their best nightly
To force alien creosote-soaked Oak
Harvested from ageless oak groves
Same groves provided masts
For Her Majesty's great ships
That carried Raleigh and Drake
Pirates brash abuse of merchant ships

Bolstered royal coffers
Established Britain in the dark corners
Of crude maps
So "The sun never sets on the Empire"

Outside Ettersberg

Inside the gates of Buchenwald
A blackened stump
Is all that remains
Of Goethe's Oak

Branches that once
Cast welcome shade
A symbol of art and honor
A place for poets

It stood at the center
Of the camp
It's loveliness and spirit tarnished
It's reverence stained
Roots drenched with lost innocence

Cries of the tortured
Bodies and spirits
Humiliated by skulled and cross-boned
Supermen in jack boots
Willingly malignant

A haven desecrated
Turned pillory and gallows
Branches bent by bodies hanged
Foreshadowed gas showers
Ovens to reduce humans
To smoke and ashes

Wagnerian marches
Nietzschean myth
Clicking heals and Heil Hitlers
Drown memory of poetry and music
Over-soul turned victim
Nature moans

Aerial bombs.
Turn Goethe's Oak to ash and smoke
To a blackened stump
Emblem of numberless people
Cremated to hide atrocities

On November Eleventh in England People Still Wear Red Paper Poppies

The eleventh hour of the eleventh day of the eleventh month marks the signing of the Armistice, 1918, to signal the end of World War One. At 11 am on 11 November 1918 the guns of the Western Front fell silent after more than four years continuous warfare.

In England people still wear red paper poppies
      on the lapels of their heavy winter coats
      in memory of the war dead.
It's been almost a hundred years
      since young boys,
      naïve and full of wonder
      crossed the Channel to die in trenches.
For the English, WWI was the "war to end all wars"—
      a global conflict fought to protect
      all future generations from the horrors of war.
Kipling, the teller of tales, was its champion—
      he "put his money where his mouth was"—
      and sent his myopic son, Jack,
      who he believed was destined to be a solider.
Like many fresh-faced lads
      with bright eyes and rosy cheeks,
      armored in good British wool the color of rich green dales,
      Jack bravely took his place in the columns
      marching grimly to the dark soggy gashes cut deep in
      farmland to face other young boys in different uniforms
      equally confused and scared and hoping for a future beyond
      the battlefield.
Their fate foreshadowed by the grim black skies
      made colder and darker with sleet
      which blew into their faces like white missiles
      by north winds roaring across the English Channel.

Jack suffered less than others,
     not because of who he was
     but because of where he was—
     he didn't last a week.
When I was a boy
     Americans wore poppies too
     sold on street corners and at store fronts
     but I can hardly remember
     the last time I saw one on a lapel or in a buttonhole.
In England poppies remind people not to forget
     the losses and sorrow brought on by war
     and its high cost of lost innocence.

*Flanders Field saw some of the most concentrated and bloodiest fighting of the First World War. There was complete devastation. Amidst the death and destruction, with the coming of spring poppies pushed through the shell pocked ground—a sign of life and hope in an otherwise grim landscape.

Poppies seeds can lie in the ground for years without germinating, and only grow after the ground has been disturbed.

Door Gunner

Her love for him was painful
        since the war,
It has been a constant deep ache
        sometimes at night he would cry out

I'm a door gunner on a helicopter
        this is how the first letter began
that made her feel safe
        after he came back he told her
(matter-of-factly)
I have killed hundreds of men
        the grunts out tramping through the jungle
Would engage call for air support
        that part was easy
from the air we couldn't see
        who was being killed
when it was over
        it was almost as if it hadn't happened
a dream

According to all accounts
        door gunners died with regularity
but she didn't know that

We got shot down once
        one second I was bullshittin' with the copilot
the next he slumped over blood everywhere
        we dropped in a rice patty
The jungle came alive
        like hell opened
vomiting up those bile yellow bastards
        it was like Christmas

gooks all wanted their part of the American dream
        I was shooting
the noise of dying filled my ears
        it filled the whole earth

Her mind clouded

At first I just shot blind
        like a crazy man
the longer I shot
        the more I wanted to see them die
I wanted to see their eyes
        mostly I wanted them to see me

Body Count

They married young
Her parents were against it
He was barely 19 when he received
Greetings from Uncle Sam
He wrote regularly

Cronkite's voice echoed
Nightly body counts on the six o'clock news
The baby slept quietly in the pink crib
She rested her head against the window
The glass was cold
Late March rain ran down in little torrents
She shivered
But it wasn't just the cold

In her hand was a
Photograph of her husband
He was atop of a pile of dead human bodies
Twisted bodies of dead VC
Many looking no older than her little brother
Their eyes empty staring off at eternity
Grinning rifle in hand
His one gold tooth seemed to sparkle
He struck the pose of the great white hunter
On the back of the snapshot were the words
116 dead gooks a record

Smiles

        I hate to see the sun goes behind the clouds she said
the gray crept through the locked windows
seeping into the very soul the house

        He grunted don't make no difference
ever since he came home from the war
nothing made a difference

        When the sun hides flowers seem to die—
the colors fade she said

        Things die when it's sunny too
I've seen it
she'd heard him say that before
when he'd talk to other men about the war
that was the only time he'd smile

        We'd lay down some smoke
those damn VC would crawl under ground—
we leave the jungle
looking like a harvested wheat field

        Totally clean
except for the bodies of those they couldn't hide
they'd bloat all up
from the sun beating down on them
days later we walk out in the jungle

        We'd shoot the really swollen ones
their yellow skin would split
gas would whistle out and stink up the air
some would sort of explode he laughed

She cried his sullenness was killing her
sucking away her soul
talk of killing was his only joy

Though sometimes he'd turn
and smile at her for no reason

The Chickens Ran

Screams are quiet now
Sun shines
Most of the world is happy
The war's 20 years gone
I can still hear it
Real and loud drifting in and out
Villagers lined up
Close to a well
Chickens ran cockeyed between their legs
Old woman cried
Babbled in a strange stupid tongue
Children close to their mothers
Stare sadly at Americans with guns and cigarettes
And savage smiles out of place on young men
The men of the village
Jabbered waving their arms
Shaking their heads
Begging us for their lives
And the villagers in unison cowered
At his rage "all the slopes are the enemy"
We kill the enemy men first
That's what men at war do
We drag them from the village howling pleading—
The wails of the women the sadness of the children
And the snapping of our M-16s drifted to heaven
And as darkness came
We led the women and children in the footsteps of the dead

June Brings Memories of War

June bring memories
Pleasant as wildflowers
Spring is a time for life
A time to tell stories fifty years old

War is the story of people
Life intermeshed
Pulled together and torn apart
The stories of wars past
Shape the stories yet to come—
Unknown to each other
Enemies only because of geography
And poor timing

War is not personal
For most of those who fight
It's a chore like weeding fields or tending cows
A most deadly work
Where the ground is flooded with blood

Billy bored with life in the middle
Of America
Handsome boy six-feet tall
Just from high school
His breath smelling of chocolate milk shakes
His world late night air after dances

In December 1942
The music stopped with the sound of bombs
Bombs made from American scrap metal
Still bearing the imprint made in America
Came crashing down on Pearl Harbor
Explosions felt clear to Kansas

Across the globe
Takeo learning language
Wondering about university halls
Felt the same rumblings
(The ones that shook Kansas)
Was called by his emperor
To a losing cause
Yet true to tradition he followed the chant
May the emperor live a thousand years

Joe just married
And already in uniform
Left high school early
The son of a widow
One of five she tried to feed
During depression years
His young wife
Left to pray
As he explored jungle paths
Eyeing the ground for tripwires
And other hidden dangers

Egos the son of a soldier
On the Russian front
Heard it on the radio
13 and proud to be a Nazi
Proud to go to war
Too proud to listen to his mother's wisdom
Left for France
His father already dead in Russia

These boys each saw death
With all its face
Turning the earth
Into tangles of waste
Women and children
Taken by errant bombs
Dropped from near where God lives

Devil's Peak

Blencathra is one of the grandest objects in Lakeland...
—Alfred Wainwright

Autumn when the hills
Are dusty green, and unless there's rain
The becks have lost
The music of water dancing lightly
Through rocky beds
Icy silver light
Of the full moon
Moves slowly from the east
Its crystal fingers
Reach deep into vales
Of the northern hills
To pull itself higher in the sky

Nighttime's shadows
Sink deeper and stretch across
Wild moorland
As moonbeams crawl slowly up
The eastern flanks of Carrick Fell
And spill over
To bathe the six summits of Blencathra
And make the serrations of the Hall Fell Ridge
Peak like a newly sharpened crosscut

And sometimes, when things are just right
The deep darkness and tomblike quiet
Is broken by the rush of wind
As the phantom army pulls up
Agitated from rocky dales and thunders
Across the side-hill
Then vanishes into the north Cumbria sky

Few see the ghostly heralds
Or hear their pipes
Or feel the explosion of hundreds of hoofs
Which cause the earth
To shake under the awful weight
Of battle-ready warriors
Who seek to wet their swords
With the blood of invisible infidels

At Play in the Fields of the Dead

Good fences make good neighbors...
                    —Robert Frost

Row by row
Stone markers stand silent
Necropolis of trimmed grass
Grid of black tarmac
Streets with names
Plot numbers addresses
Eastman and Amos
Davis and Dickerson
Engraved with crosses and Stars of David
Marked as Masons or Eastern Star
Woodsmen of the World
Knights of Columbus
But mostly dates
1802–1875 or 1914–1950
1952–1973 or 1895–1918
A roll call of generations
Soldiers surgeons fathers farmers
Mothers sisters sons and daughters
Rest under outstretched arms
Blue Spruce cottonwoods
And brown of late winter grass
Upswept leaves
Flashes of pink and yellow
Plastic flowers survived winter's snow
Surrounded by quiet and birdsong
Magpies hop between the headstones
Blast away a blur black and white
Solitary American flag marks
A soldier's grave
On the east a ditch cuts
Behind this city of the dead
A subdivision of gray marble crypts

Line its banks
In this neighborhood
Everyone knows their place
No loud quarrels or gossip
Pinecones and leaves fall where they may
No fences only trees grass
And withered leaves.

At Flag Fen

Yesterday

Warriors' retired weapons
"Beat swords to ploughshares
Spears to pruning hooks"
Cast murderous relics
In shallow graves of brown peat
Broken swords
Spearheads from shafts
Smashed helmets
Shields twisted

Today

Silver rods quiver
Pull at primitive secrets
She looks up
And to no one in particular
Prays

Someday

The Somme, 1916

Different, this day

Ten–thousand times,

Fifteen hundred cannons shower earth

Shrapnel violates

Khaki and grey uniforms

Shatters bodies blinds eyes stains souls,

Bombs moan through clouds

Sun masked in black smoke

Fields turned mud

Confused Meadow Larks and Doves

Shrill screams go unheard,

Blood colors poppies

Drips through layers of torn flesh

Mingles with chalk dust,

God-mocked gas chokes lungs

Earth groans.

The Massacre of Innocents 1914–1917

Death held no wonder.
            —Wade Davis

Older men declare war. But it is youth that must fight and die.
                        —Herbert Hoover

In Toronto
St. Paul's gray walls
Hold Books of Remembrance
Roster of the dead
Fresh-faced boys
Queens Own Rifles
Lost "Racing to the Sea"

Young eyes dead lights
Search the heavens
Of Passchendaele
Body parts mashed in mud
Of "no man's land"
Trenches gas-filled graves
Scarecrows crucified on barbed wire
Others blasted to nothing
For King and Country

War is political poetry
Calligraphy of bullet holes
Scribed on adolescent chests
Turning young hope
To obscene art
Pornography of progress

In the holy cavern
Footfall echoes
Candles flicker
Shadows dance
Sorrow hides in cracks and corners
Tears stain floors
Of the regimental church

From Atop Westminster

Oliver Cromwell's head
      Found a way home
      After twenty-seven years.
Blown from atop Westminster
      Cast about for centuries
      Carnival to freak show
Hidden in haystack or cellar
      Red hair mostly worn away
      Telltale mole above vacant sockets
Leathered skin stretches tight across the jaw
      Lord Protector honored as a king
      Three years in the Abbey floor
Aside poets and priests
      Kings orders—exhume
      Treason exposed
Public execution after the fact
      Death or grave affords no guarantee
      Time unable to protect or hide naked shame

Vale of Tears

Oh, cruel was the snow that sweeps Glencoe
And covers the grave o'Donald
Oh, cruel was the foe that raped Glencoe
And murdered the house of MacDonald
                    —From "Ballad of Glencoe"

In the spring the heather-covered hills,
Are carpeted with tiny purple flowers
And yellow gorse explodes up the hillside
The rugged mountains soar skyward
In the vale stones are abundant,
And small streams, called burns,
Gently flow through the peaty moors.
Thick-wooled highland sheep graze
Under great rock faces
And the matted bracken turns green from brown.
The Clachaig Inn stands immaculate white
Against the deep green of Glencoe.
Was not always so.
In the bitter darkness of February*
Before the sun could climb above the Tree Sisters
Cruel orders from King William,
"Murder under trust"
Rested in the stony hearts of the Campbell's
Who safe-harbored with the MacDonald's
Against the rages of Scottish winter
And awaited the deadly signal.
When it came seventy-eight died
The thirty-eight men by the sword
While forty women and children
Were driven from burning homes
Into the bleak winter morning.
It's been said "that time heals all"
But here in the stormy Highlands
Even after nearly four hundred years
There are no words of comfort.

* The Massacre of Glencoe occurred in the early morning of February 13, 1692. The massacre began simultaneously in three settlements along the glen—Invercoe, Inverrigan, and Achacon—although the killing took place all over the glen as fleeing MacDonalds were pursued. The guests, led by members of the Clan Campbell, who had accepted hospitality from the MacDonalds as a subterfuge for their murderous plans. The attacks were intended as an example.

Sniper: With, or Without Warning

Death came today,
Without warning, swift and silent—
Yet, I find it hard to believe that Death
Comes without some pain,
Or in complete silence, without a warning of some sort
Maybe like a bright flash—
(Joyce called such phenomena Epiphany,
A revelation, a preview of eternity).
Something as important as the proverbial "Last Judgment"
Must be heralded, at least be announced.
Even the Bible speaks of Gabriel sounding the Trump
Bringing about the end of time.
But "the end of time" is relative—isn't it?
What is death—does it come like a lightning bolt,
Without what we call a warning?
Is it like an old man dropping out of mortality
While walking in the hills or out of a church?
Or does it like to come best in the deep quiet of night
While all the World is sleeping; that depends.
It will visit all of us,
Either now or later, but it is inevitable.
No one can escape it
I think I know what it means when I read John Donne's
"No man is an island"
Or "ask not for whom the bell tolls."
Inside, just a little fear pricks my heart—an implication?
"Sinner in the hands of an angry God."
While my mother lay in the hospital
Waiting for the cancer to take her,
Her brother, attempting to comfort, to say the "right things,"
To mitigate her fear of death.
He said "I could go tomorrow, dying does not scare me."
Yet it wasn't him with all those tubes in his arms
Flushing away all sensation with narcotics

Waiting in a haze for the vale to part.
He had a tee time in his immediate future
With no angels hovering about the tee box on the first hole
Hoping to guide him toward the light.
No, you'll never make me believe death can surprise—
Why would it sneak up on us?
After all, it does have complete control—
It's its nature.
It can deliver its message, invitation or eviction notice,
At any time, with, or without warning.

Mud, Gas, and Poppies

Man may be excused for feeling some pride at having risen, though not through his own exertions, to the very summit of the organic scale; and the fact of his having thus risen, instead of having been aboriginally placed there, may give him hope for a still higher destiny in the distant future.
—Charles Darwin

Mustard gas
Flood trenches
Soldiers drown as in flooded seas
Urine masks to thwart chlorine gas
Gummy mask
Human genius for murder
Plum pudding bombs
Trench art
Lice fleas scabies
Huns
Flame throwers
Forests shattered by canon fire
Earth matted and pocked scared
Poppies red as blood
Military insanity
Executions
Verdun
Mud
No man's land deadly expanse between trenches
Join the buffs hunt the Huns
The church send the Irish to war paradox
War King George V
Welsh miners tunnel
July 1, 1916 blows mile long trench no deaths
Capt. Billie Neville
Soccer ball
Amputations

Murder of innocence
Cigarettes mask the rot of the dead
Passchendaele 250,000 dead
In one mile

When the World Ends

When the world ends
will it be overrun by tanks
like Armadillos
the sting of a Manticore's
Scorpion tail
Or ancient creatures resurrected
from test tubes
Possibly pregnant clouds
drift silently
dropping poison
makes snow sparkle
waters turn deadly black
Earth suffocated because
forests cut clear
by greed
What about those
who come after us

About the Author

Mikel Vause holds a Ph.D. from Bowling Green University and is a Brady Presidential Distinguish Professor at Weber State University. He is the author of numerous articles, poems, and short stories and is the author or editor of six books. His poetry collections are: *I Knew It Would Come to This; At the Edge of Things; Looking for the Old Crown; The Scent of Juniper; Secondly Sources;* and *A Most Terrible and Deadly Season.* In 2016 he was a Pushcart Prize nominee for his poem "What said the Thunder."

www.ingramcontent.com/pod-product-compliance
Lightning Source LLC
Chambersburg PA
CBHW022015080426
42733CB00007B/613